FUN FACTS

Ripley's
Believe It or Not!®
Kids

& SILLY STORIES

ACTIVITY ANNUAL 2017

What's Inside?

Silly Stories!

Games & Puzzles Galore!

Terrific Travels!

A Tasty Recipe!

Page 65

Page 80

Check THIS Out

REALLY?
Giant moose sculpture

NO WAY!
Dog-shaped hotel

Fantastic Festivals!

Unbelievable Facts!

CUTE
Road for ducks

Page 25

CRAZY
Flip-flop creations

Page 74

WOW!
Pink sand beaches

Don't Forget to Pack

YOUR PASSPORT!

German citizens are allowed to stick out their tongues in their passport photos!

A LUGGAGE LOCK!

Alan Freed collected over 11,000 lost or broken luggage locks while working at a Washington, DC, USA, airport, later using them to create a giant padlock weighing over 130 kilograms!

SUNGLASSES!

Bagel the cat, born without eyelids, wears glasses to protect her eyes!

MONEY!

He Peiqi of Chongqing City, China, built a replica of his hometown using over 50,000 coins! He didn't use a drop of glue!

A SWEATER!

An animal sanctuary in England knits woolly winter sweaters for its chickens! Hundreds of bald birds are now warm through the colder months thanks to the 'chi-kinis'.

JEANS!

No one loves denim more than British artist Ian Berry, better known as Denimu. He carefully cuts, stitches, arranges, and pastes the panels into awesome urban landscapes.

Worldwide Whirly Word

Can you find all 15 cities hidden in this puzzle? Make sure to look up, down, backward, across, and diagonally!

ATHENS

BEIJING

MADRID

BERLIN

CAIRO

PARIS

NEW YORK

JEDDAH

NAIROBI

LONDON

TOKYO

ROME

TORONTO

TUNIS

LIMA

P	J	R	F	Q	L	Z	B	L	Q	U	F	G	I	A
J	E	D	D	A	H	O	I	Z	A	E	K	J	H	I
E	L	D	T	M	G	M	N	W	M	U	W	K	S	L
A	C	U	M	H	A	N	O	D	G	M	O	T	I	X
S	Q	E	A	L	W	E	X	F	O	R	U	B	O	A
T	Z	U	D	W	S	W	S	A	I	N	O	E	H	N
J	U	M	R	K	N	Y	P	A	Q	R	K	I	I	B
T	T	Q	I	D	B	O	C	G	I	N	N	J	D	R
F	O	X	D	E	Z	R	L	A	A	H	W	I	R	O
M	T	K	R	T	N	K	N	E	D	T	Q	N	E	R
L	G	L	Y	S	F	T	T	Z	B	V	H	G	V	K
Q	I	P	P	O	D	K	U	P	W	U	I	E	N	P
N	E	M	O	R	M	W	N	F	K	J	J	Q	N	Z
T	O	R	O	N	T	O	I	P	D	B	P	I	S	
P	A	R	I	S	A	C	S	X	A	B	A	F	A	D

Want to check
your answers?
Turn to page 88
for the puzzle solution!

At Hotel Costa Verde, in Costa Rica's Manuel Antonio National Park, guests can stay in a 1965 Boeing 727 airplane that juts 15 metres into the jungle's canopy!

Weird Hotels

Located at the foot of China's Emei Mountain, the Haoduo Panda Hotel is unbearably cute, from the panda-themed rooms to the employees' uniforms – giant panda suits!

Hoisted 45 metres above Harlingen Harbour in The Netherlands, guests at the Crane Hotel can rotate their room 360 degrees!

The two-storey-tall Dog Bark Park Inn in Cottonwood, Idaho, USA, is built in the shape of a beagle! Pets are welcome, too!

TAIJI

Tea is always served with a twist at the Taiji Tea Ceremony House in Hangzhou, China. A Chinese acrobat will perform an ancient tai chi tea ceremony where he will bend over backward to prepare your tea, and then pour it into your cup – upside down!

TEA HOUSE

Up Pup and Away!

Woody, Helena, Holly, and Oban are four special guide dogs in England that help their partially sighted owners manoeuvre through airports and travel on planes. After their training, the dogs 'graduated' by taking their first flight!

Afraid of flying? Therapy dogs at Charlotte Douglas International Airport in North Carolina, USA, help tense travellers relax with inviting 'Pet Me' signs.

Milo, a six-year-old terrier from Cardiff, Wales, acts as a guide dog for his older brother, Eddie, a blind Labrador retriever.

Animal ROUND-UP

Can you find all ten differences between the suitcases? Have fun packing for your pet!

Are we there YET?

14

BONUS:
Spot the teeny tiny poisonous frog in the picture below.

Can you find the six differences between the two scenes? Colour in the differences.

Every October on the feast day of the Patron Saint of Animals, Saint Francis of Assisi, pets all over the world are blessed by priests!

Want to check your answers?
Turn to page 88 for the puzzle solutions!

Rare Runways

Barra, Scotland, is home to the world's only scheduled beach–landing airport. Flights are dictated by the tide!

Singapore's Changi Airport boasts a butterfly garden with over 1,000 butterflies!

There is an 18-hole golf course sandwiched between the runways at Thailand's Don Muang International Airport!

Winging It

Flying It

Get ready for takeoff! Here's **ten** first-class **facts** about aeroplanes!

The longest flight in the world is about 13,679 kilometres from Sydney, Australia, to Dallas, Texas, USA – around **17 hours!**

There are **5,000** aeroplanes in the sky above the United States at any given time!

Flying through a thunderstorm can expose aeroplane passengers to radiation levels equivalent to 400 chest X-rays!

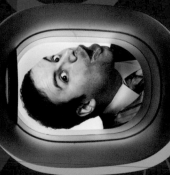

Bar Nunn, Wyoming, USA, was the top of an airport in 1982. The old runways now serve as streets!

English is the international language of flight. All flight staff are required to speak English.

The runway at Gisborne Airport in New Zealand has

The Boeing® aeroplane plant in Washington State, USA, is so huge that Disneyland® could fit inside!

A plane going from Australia to Malaysia made an emergency landing when the 2,186 sheep in the cargo bay passed too much gas.

About 1 in 5 people have some fear of flying, or 'aviophobia'.

The world's shortest commercial flight – between the Westray and Papa Westray Orkney Islands – can be completed in just 47 seconds!

Selfie Sidekicks

Allan Dixon from Ireland is a real-life Dr Dolittle — he's been able to 'talk' over 30 different animal species from around the world into posing for a selfie!

Your Odd Adventure

How many smaller words can you make out of the letters in the word below? Words must have four letters or more.

Want to check your answers? Turn to page 89 for the puzzle solutions!

A D V E N T U R E

_____ _____

_____ _____

_____ _____

_____ _____

_____ _____

Ask a friend to give you words...

...to fill in the blanks in this story...

...but don't let them peek!

On the _____ trip to _____ , my _____ friend
          adjective   place   adjective

and I decided to play a game. It was a very _____ trip, so we
                                              adjective

wanted to play a game with _____ and _____ . Using
                            plural noun   plural noun

our _____ to _____ , we tried to get the _____
     noun   verb   plural noun

next to us to play along, but they just _____ at us and
                                          action verb

_____ away. After a few rounds, we thought the game could
action verb

use some _____ so we turned on the _____ and
          plural noun   noun

started _____ to the _____ that came on. This
         action verb   noun

lasted for _____ before I got _____ and
            measurement of time   adjective

decided to _____ . When we got hungry, we _____
            action verb   action verb

our _____ and ate _____ with _____ for
     noun   noun   noun

dessert. We will never _____ that trip. It was the _____
                        verb   adjective

trip of my _____ !
            noun

Now, read it out loud!

23

Weird Festivals

Shhh...

Ocean City, New Jersey, USA, holds a 'Quiet Festival' every November, where attractions include kite-flying and sign language.

Each year, Toyohashi, Japan, hosts an extreme fire festival! People set off huge homemade bamboo fireworks that explode just inches from their faces.

On the first Sunday of every September, the Bloemencorso, or flower parade, makes its way through the streets of the Dutch town of Zundert.

25

Train Travel

In Kobe, Japan, tiny 'tunnels' were built for turtles to cross the train tracks safely.

Eugene Bostick of Fort Worth, Texas, USA, built a custom train to take his rescue pups for a ride!

All aboard!

Nitama, a cat, is the stationmaster of the Kishi train station in Japan! Her beloved predecessor, Tama, was even enshrined as a goddess!

The London underground has its own distinct subspecies of mosquito – *Culex pipiens molestus!*

From 1992 to 2012, the waste from New York City, USA, rode on a special 'poop train' to Colorado, USA, for farmers to use on crops!

Mo's Bows!

Fourteen-year-old Moziah Bridges started his own bow tie company, Mo's Bows! Moziah has even given President Obama a custom Obama Blue bow tie, and he also served as an ESPN® fashion correspondent in 2015, and an up-and-coming basketball star wore his bow tie!

Moziah tied up the loose ends we had
about the bow tie biz!

· ·

Q: How do you balance running a business
with your schoolwork?

A: Well, I'm homeschooled, so I usually just do
schoolwork at the beginning of the day, and
my company work at the end of the day.

Q: Who would you most love to give a bow tie to?

A: I would love to give my ties to Kanye West –
he's someone in both the fashion world and
music world.

Q: What advice would you give young people
dreaming of creating their own business?

A: Invest in yourself, and really take time to
think about what you want to achieve in
life – and make sure it makes you smile at
the end of the day.

Crafty

A group of artists called Taxi Fabric are transforming taxis in Mumbai, India, into works of art. Everything from the doors to the steering wheel is covered in colourful designs!

Art on the GO!

The night before an Indian bride gets married, the palms of her hands and feet are often painted with amazing henna patterns. Henna has been used to colour skin and hair for over 5,000 years!

1 Henna comes from the henna plant.

2 The leaves are crushed and made into a paste, which is applied to the skin in a cool design.

3 Once the henna is applied, it is left to dry for around 20 minutes.

Design your own henna patterns on this hand.

4 The top layer then peels off, revealing the beautiful design underneath.

Follow the tyre tracks to find out which crafty cab makes it to the Taj Mahal!

Kanyakumari Beach

Taj Mahal

Hawa Mahal

Khari Baoli

Want to check your answers? Turn to page 89 for the puzzle solution!

The Taj Mahal is a white marble mausoleum considered one of the Seven Wonders of the World.

Think

Lobster Larry
Sitting in the small town of Kingston SE, Australia, is Larry the lobster - a massive metal crustacean more than 15 metres high!

Mac the Moose
A giant sculpture of a moose welcomes visitors to Moose Jaw, Saskatchewan, Canada. He's more than three storeys high!

This page is a-moose-ing!

Big!

Don't be so corny!

Field of Corn
In Dublin, Ohio, USA, a former cornfield now houses 109 people-sized ears of concrete corn in one huge, weird art display.

Kelpies
Falkirk in Scotland is home to The Kelpies, the largest equine sculpture in the world at 30 metres high!

Make Way!

Ducks live on canals across England. To encourage walkers and cyclists to share the roads, special lanes were labelled for feathered friends only.

The 42.7-metres-tall Eshima Ohashi bridge in Japan offers a thrill ride on the open road. It's known as the 'rollercoaster bridge' for its steep incline.

In 1831, Nancy Kerlin Barnett was buried on a hill in Amity, Indiana, USA. Nancy's grandson never let the county build a road over her grave, so her tombstone still stands – in the middle of the road!

37

In December 2015, a church in Berlin, Germany, hosted a *Star Wars*-themed church service!

FAR FAR AWAY

Scenes on the ice planet Hoth in *The Empire Strikes Back* were really that brutally cold - they were shot on location at the Hardangerjøkulen glacier in Norway during a storm!

HI-SEAS

In Mauna Loa, Hawaii, six volunteer 'astronauts' live in a solar-powered dome for a whole year and test space equipment for NASA.

Igor the drone

By living in the Hawaii Space Exploration Analog and Simulation mission (HI-SEAS), they are getting a taste of what life on Mars might be like!

This is an inside view of the HI-SEAS dome. In the main area, the crew eats, works, exercises, and grows plants.

Pets in Space

Is it a bird? Is it a plane? No, it's Daisy, the spectacular flying Chihuahua. Daisy's owner, James Holmdahl of Bend, Oregon, USA, attached his pup to a cluster of helium balloons during the town's Fourth of July Parade!

Welcome to the

The entire Amazon River Basin once flowed in the opposite direction!

Since 2002, scientific expeditions in the Amazon rainforest have revealed 10 new species of bioluminescent mushrooms!

Jungle

The beetle *Agra sasquatch* of the Amazon rainforest is named after Bigfoot because of its large feet!

To help capture its prey, the margay, an Amazonian wildcat, mimics the calls of small tamarin monkeys.

Rainforest Round-Up!

Draw creepy creatures and things you might come across on an Amazonian swim. Don't forget disgusting leeches, snakes, piranhas, and chilling crocodiles!

Rainforests contain more than half of the world's plant and animal species.

Learn more about the amazing rainforests with this fun *crossword puzzle!*

Want to check your answers? Turn to page 89 for the puzzle solution!

ACROSS

2 A chart of the rivers, mountains, and streams of an area

4 A tropical forest

6 The protection of animals, plants, and natural resources

10 A tool for finding direction whose needle points north

11 Having a lot of moisture in the air

DOWN

1 An area with a lot of rain and very tall trees

3 Something that protects an animal by making it hard to see

5 Having a high temperature

7 An animal or plant that is very rare and might die out completely

8 A river in South America

9 Relating to the tropics

47

Flip-Flop Fun!

Ocean Sole® in Nairobi, Kenya, has found a way to recycle flip-flops by creating handmade toys, necklaces, and even life-sized sculptures!

RIPLEY'S Asks...

We asked Ocean Sole's Joe Mwakiremba about this rubbish-to-treasure company.

....

Q: What was the inspiration to use the flip-flops to make toys?

A: Our founder, Julie Church, observed some children on the island of Kiwayu were making toys out of the flip-flop debris that washed up on the beaches.

Q: How do the flip-flops end up on the beaches?

A: Some are washed away during rainy seasons, and some are carried by ocean currents from as far as Indonesia, creating rubbish patches in our oceans.

Illuminated Igloos

Stay cozy and warm in a heated glass igloo at the Kakslauttanen Arctic Resort in Finland!

Through the igloo's clear ceiling, the colourful aurora borealis, also known as the northern lights, will flash across the night sky as you drift off to sleep.

Do You Wanna Build a Snow Globe?

No two snowflakes are the same.

California

GEORGIA

The largest snowball fight on record took place in Saskatchewan, Canada, with exactly 7,681 snow fighters!

Stuff you need:

- A small, clean glass jar with a lid
- A small plastic toy or figurine—choose one you aren't tempted to play with
- 1-2 tsp glitter
- Clean water
- Glue
- Paper towel

Here we'll craft, and here we'll play!

1. Glue and stick your plastic toy or figurine to the inside of the jar lid. Place the lid on a paper towel and let the glue dry completely.

2. Next, fill your jar with water and add glitter to the water.

3. Carefully apply glue along the inside rim of the jar's lid. Be careful not to smear any extra glue onto your figurine.

4. Screw the lid on top of the jar and set it aside - right side up - on the paper towel until the glue dries completely.

5. That's it! Shake your jar or tip it upside down to make it snow! (The cold never bothered you anyway!)

Go on a Polar Expedition

Start at the penguins' home at the bottom of the page and battle through the maze to the fish, avoiding the cracks in the ice. Then try to get back, but this time avoid the seals instead!

TIP!
Use different colours for the journey to the sea and the journey home again.

HOME

Today _____ and I finally _____ to Antarctica! The
          person   *verb ending in -ed*

trip was so _____ that we _____ during dinner
              adjective   *verb ending in -ed*

the first night. Thankfully, we managed to pack enough _____
                                                          noun

and _____ for our three-day hike. It was so _____ we
      noun   *adjective*

could not feel our _____ ! We saw some _____ and _____,
                     noun   *animal*   *animal*

and they were so _____ and _____ ! Suddenly, I fell in
                   adjective   *adjective*

some cold _____ , so _____ had to help me _____
             noun   *person*   *verb*

my _____. The best part was _____ the _____
     noun   *verb ending in -ing*   *noun*

every night by the fire. Before we left, I _____ the
                                             verb ending in -ed

sled dogs and said goodbye to our _____ guide. I hope
                                      adjective

we'll _____ in _____ for another polar expedition!
        verb   *year*

**Ask friends to choose words
to** fill in the blanks in this
story, **but don't let them peek.**
Then, read it out loud!

**Want to check
your answers?**
Turn to page 89
for the puzzle solution!

Capybara Cutie

Meet Sweetie – style icon, Internet celebrity, and a capybara, one of the world's largest rodents! This glamourous gal can be spotted window shopping and greeting fans in her hometown of Las Vegas, Nevada, USA.

Ripley's Asks...

Emily told us more about her pet capybara!

....

Q: Sweetie is quite the fashionista. What are some of her favourite outfits?

A: She loves her tutus, dinosaur onesies, animal costumes, and hoodies!

Q: Sweetie is also an animal activist – what's her mission?

A: In some countries, capybaras are hunted, eaten, and used for leather. I hope that through social media, people get to know her and understand these are kind and loving animals who are friends, not food!

I just love pink!

Creature

Europe's kings and queens used to give each other rare and exotic animals as gifts. In the UK, these animals were known as the Royal Menagerie of England, and they lived in the Tower of London for over 600 years!

In 1811, the Hudson Bay Company gave the first grizzly bear ever seen in England to King George III, who named it Martin.

T ORS' GATE

Collection

In 1828, General Watson gave King George IV a Bengal lion called George as a gift.

Many beasts and fowl called the Tower of London home in 1829, including these crazy critters:

an African porcupine

baboons

a brown coati

a caracal

cheetahs

eagles

elephants

emus

a jaguar

kangaroos

leopards

lions, tigers, and bears

llamas

an ocelot

a paradoxorus

a puma

a secretary bird

hundreds of snakes

a striped hyena

white-headed mongooses

a zebra

Paradoxorus

Food for Thought!

Zoe Fox from Leicestershire, England, spent 300 hours making a life-size tiger out of cake!

Miniature artist Enrique Ramos of Mexico City, Mexico, painted this Aztec scene on a tortilla!

The world's first hedgehog cafe opened in Tokyo, Japan, in 2016!

If you're bored of cereal and milk, maybe try a Rainbow Bagel from The Bagel Store in Brooklyn, New York!

Kid Chef!

KID CHEF ELIANA

Eliana Coo...

With grandparents from Louisiana (USA), the Philippines, Cuba, and Honduras, recipes from 15-year-old professional chef Eliana de Las Casas have an international flair!

We asked Eliana about her recipe for success!

Q: What was the first recipe you ever created, and how did it turn out?

A: When I was four years old, I created heart-shaped strawberry and cream cheese sandwiches. They were delicious, and I served them at a Valentine's Day party.

Q: What was the funniest thing that's happened while you were cooking?

A: My mom and I roasted chestnuts for the first time, but I didn't research how to roast them and just put them in the oven. Suddenly, it sounded like a popcorn machine exploded. When my mom opened the oven door, chestnuts literally flew out! We didn't know we were supposed to cut slits into the chestnuts to allow the steam to escape. Needless to say, we learned our lesson!

Q: Is there someone famous you'd love to cook for? What would you make for them?

A: I would love to prepare for Ed Sheeran, my favourite musician, a traditional Louisiana meal of jambalaya, gumbo, and shrimp étouffée, with pralines as a sweet treat.

Let's Get Cooking!

An Internet star since she was eight, Eliana's YouTube cooking tutorials led to her own web radio show and three award-winning cookbooks. Try making Eliana's delicious pizza recipe!

TWO-INGREDIENT PIZZA DOUGH
(Serves 2)

Stuff you need:
- **240 millilitres self-rising flour**
- **240 millilitres Greek yoghurt**
- **olive oil**
- **baking tray**
- **medium-size bowl**
- **pizza sauce**
- **cheese**
- **toppings for pizza**

Do it yourself:
1. Preheat oven to 205°C.
2. Using the olive oil, grease a baking tray.
3. In a medium bowl, combine flour and yoghurt. Mix until it forms a ball.
4. Divide the ball in half and place on a flat, floured surface.
5. Roll out the balls to form small, circular pizzas.
6. Place on greased baking tray.
7. Drizzle a little olive oil on top.
8. Add sauce, cheese, and then toppings for pizza.
9. Bake for 20 minutes. Enjoy!

Look for Your Lunch

Hungry? Find these 15 foods from around the world. Make sure you look up, down, across, and diagonally!

CURRY

CREPE

DUMPLING

FAJITA

FETA

FLAN

FONDUE

KEBAB

KIMCHI

PIZZA

POUTINE

RAMEN

SUSHI

TACO

WASABI

```
C U R R Y L Z K L Q U I P Z A
R E D D A H O I Z A E K O H I
E L D T A C M M W M U W U W L
P C U M H B H S D G M I T I X
E Q E A A W O H S U S H I B M
T Z U B W S P I A S N O N A A
J U E R O N S P A A R K E S B
T K Q C D U M P L I N G A A R
F O A D T Z O F A A B W I W O
M T K R A M E N E A T Q N E R
L A Z Z C F T T S E U D N O F
Q C A P B F K A P W U A S N P
N W A O R E W C F K J J S U Z
P A U O N T P I Z Z A P I A S
F A J I T A C S X A B T A C W
```

Peas look carefully!

Want to check your answers? Turn to page 89 for the puzzle solution!

Monumental Madness

The Great Wall of China was built with earth, stones, and RICE!

It took over 1,000 elephants to carry the materials used to build the Taj Mahal.

Nailed it.

It is illegal to take a photograph of the Eiffel Tower at night.

But first, let me take a selfie!

The Statue of Liberty has a 1.4 metre long nose and an 2.4 metre long index finger!

Clap your hands in front of Chichen Itza's El Castillo pyramid, and the echo will sound like a chirping bird.

Monumental Mazes

Finish

PYRAMID SCHEME

Make it out of the maze, but don't get trapped in the treasure rooms!

Start ➡

STONEHENGE REVENGE

Start

Find your way through the maze to get to Stonehenge!

The 40-tonne stones used to build Stonehenge were moved and positioned more than 32 kilometres without the benefit of the wheel!

Want to check your answers? Turn to page 90 for the puzzle solutions!

The World Bathtubbing Championships are a series of races where competitors kayak in a bathtub!

MOVE IT!

Every year the Ascot Races in the UK have a Lamb National, where a herd of sheep fence jump, each one with a little teddy bear jockey.

Switzerland's Mount Niesen is home to the world's longest single staircase race, known as Niesenlauf. Reaching the top is equal to climbing the Empire State Building more than seven times!

Set Sail!

Although there are over 7,000 islands, only about 2 percent of the Caribbean is inhabited!

KO-KEE, KO-KEE.

The male coqui frog of Puerto Rico is less than 5 centimetres long, but its croak is as loud as a passing jet!

The flag of the Turks and Caicos Islands mistakenly featured an igloo on it for 80 years!

The pink sand found on the beaches of Harbour Island in the Bahamas gets its colour from millions of microscopic animals with bright pink and red shells.

ACTUAL SIZE

Barbados is home to the world's smallest snake. It's just 10 centimetres long and as wide as a noodle!

Theme Park
Word Search

Can you find all 15 things hidden in this puzzle? Make sure to look up, down, backward, across, and diagonally!

CANDY FLOSS

WATER RIDE

POPCORN

DOUGHNUTS

HOT DOGS

CAROUSEL

FERRIS WHEEL

MUSIC

GAMES

BUMPER CAR

PRIZES

PARADE

FIREWORKS

TICKETS

SWEETS

76

M	J	S	D	B	L	Z	M	L	Q	U	F	G	I	G
U	E	T	O	U	H	A	I	Z	E	D	A	R	A	P
S	L	E	U	M	F	P	N	S	E	T	T	O	O	H
I	C	K	G	P	R	I	Z	E	S	M	R	P	I	W
E	A	C	H	E	P	O	P	C	O	Y	C	B	A	A
N	N	I	N	R	R	S	W	H	S	O	O	T	H	N
N	D	T	U	C	N	S	P	S	R	R	E	I	O	B
U	T	Q	T	A	B	T	O	N	I	R	N	C	T	R
S	O	X	S	R	Z	L	C	A	R	H	I	I	D	O
T	U	S	E	C	F	N	N	I	D	S	G	N	O	R
E	G	L	Y	Y	S	O	D	T	U	O	A	D	G	G
E	I	P	D	O	D	E	U	M	W	U	M	E	S	P
W	E	N	F	E	R	R	I	S	W	H	E	E	L	Z
S	A	N	N	E	L	C	A	R	O	U	S	E	L	N
C	A	N	D	I	B	S	K	R	O	W	E	R	I	F

Want to check your answers?
Turn to page 90
for the puzzle solution!

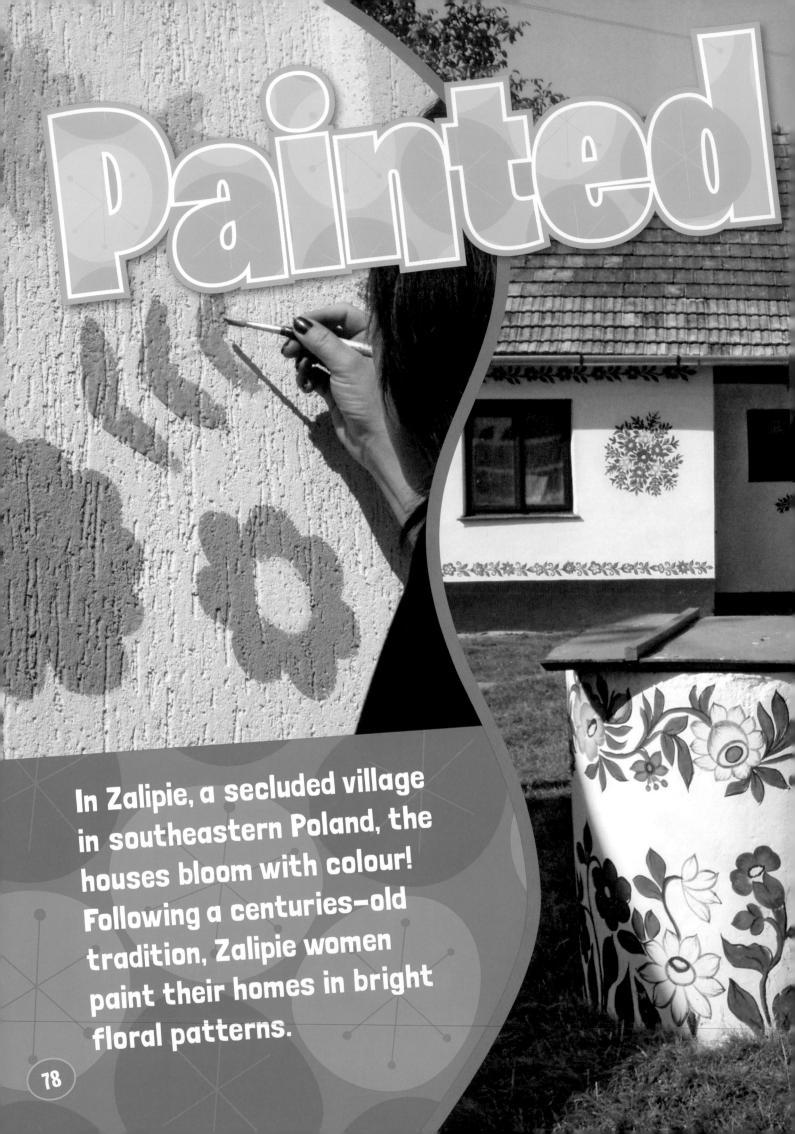

Painted

In Zalipie, a secluded village in southeastern Poland, the houses bloom with colour! Following a centuries-old tradition, Zalipie women paint their homes in bright floral patterns.

Village

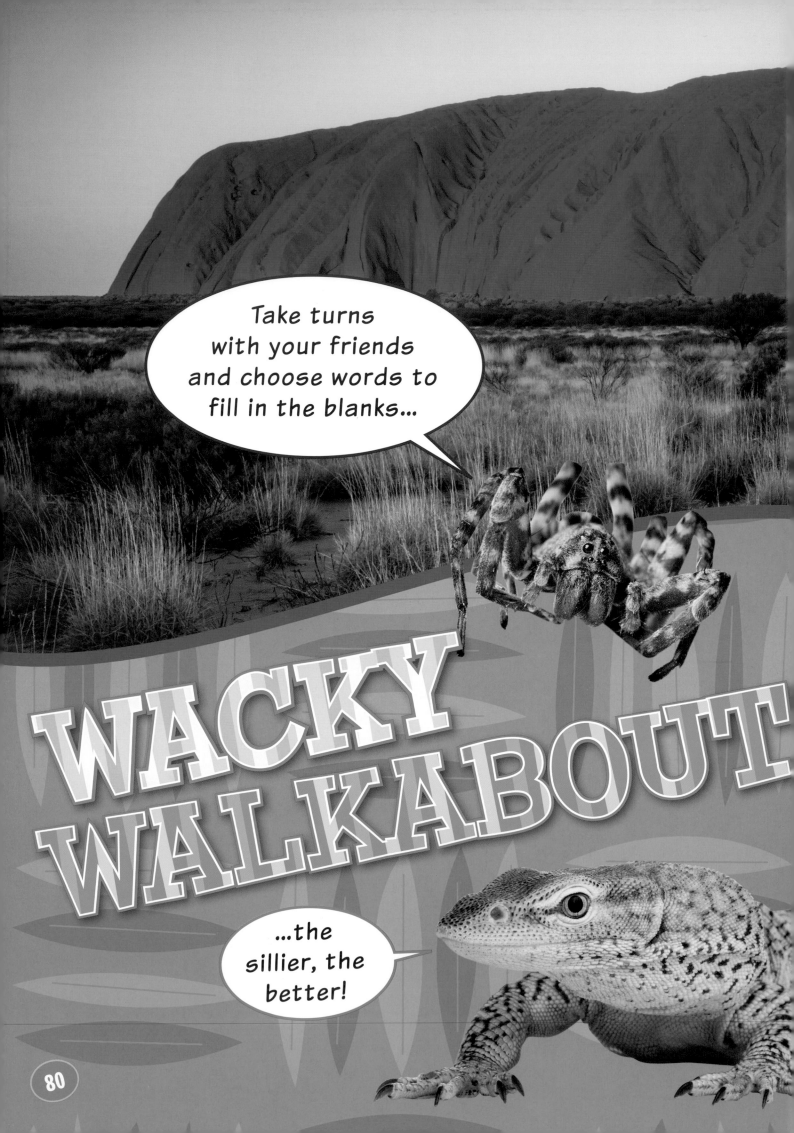

After you are done, read it out loud!

_____ and I just _____ our Australian walkabout, and
   Person   **verb ending in -ed**

it was _____! We started in the morning, _____ in the
     adjective   **verb ending in -ing**

bush with our guides. Right away we saw _____ kangaroos
                                     adjective

_____ around and _____ koalas in the trees.
verb ending in -ing   **adjective**

We even saw roaming emus. Those are _____! At times
                                       adjective

we heard _____ cockatoos in the _____ and saw monitor
        adjective   **noun**

lizards _____ under rocks and boulders. I thought we
       verb ending in -ing

would see _____, but we were not so lucky. At night we heard
        noun

some possums as they _____ for _____, and we saw fruit
               verb ending in -ed   **noun**

bats that looked like flying foxes. Finally, I got _____ by
                                             verb ending in -ed

a wolf spider! Can you believe it? The _____ hurt only a little,
                                    noun

but it was super itchy! This trip was so _____, and I can't
                                     adjective

wait to do it again!

CRAZY COUNTRIES

Russians have no word for blue - Russian has separate phrases for 'light blue' and 'dark blue', but none for 'blue'.

Two churches on the Greek island of Chios celebrate Easter by firing thousands of rockets at each other.

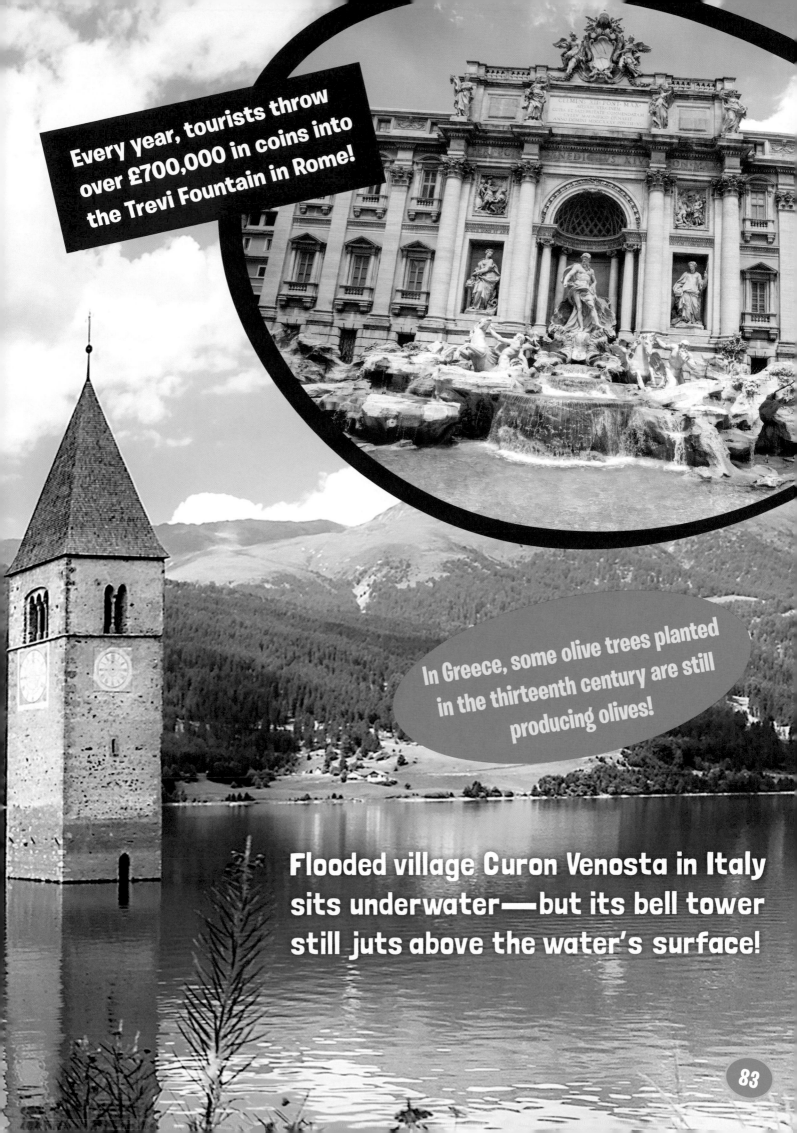

Every year, tourists throw over £700,000 in coins into the Trevi Fountain in Rome!

In Greece, some olive trees planted in the thirteenth century are still producing olives!

Flooded village Curon Venosta in Italy sits underwater—but its bell tower still juts above the water's surface!

Feathers in Flight

The wild budgerigar of Australia swarm in the thousands – even millions – when in search of food and water!

In Madison, Wisconsin, USA, the official bird is the plastic pink flamingo!

Green parakeets nest in the crater of the active Massaya Volcano in Nicaragua!

In February 2016, Lynn Campbell of Aberdeenshire, Scotland, photographed a sparrow in her garden with a very rare, abnormally large beak!

Bon Voyage!

Fill in the blanks with the correct mode of transportation. Then order the numbered letters to reveal the secret message!

1 This hovers and watches traffic.

__ __ __ __ __ __ __ __ __ __ __
                                            1 10   7

2 Glide along the tracks in this. Choo choo!

__ __ __ __
11 5 4

3 Fly in the sky on this.

__ __ __ __ __ __ __
3 12 14   9

4 Hold on tight while the dogs pull you along.

__ __ __ __
  6   8

5 Pedal and balance on this. Once you know how, you never forget.

__ __ __ __ __ __ __
13   2

UNSCRAMBLE THE SECRET MESSAGE

__ __ __ __ __ __ __ __ __ __ __ __ __ __ !
1 2 3 4 5 6 7 8 9 10 11 12 13 14

Help the lost husky find his way to the dog sled!

Want to check your answers?
Turn to page 90 for the puzzle solutions!

FROG

Your Odd Adventure, page 22

Four-letter word answers

aunt	neat		
dare	need		
dart	rate		
date	rent		
deer	tear		
duet	tree		
even	true		
ever	vent		

Five-letter word answers

averted	tender
deter	trade
eater	tundra
enter	under
nature	unread
never	veteran
raven	
tavern	

Art on the GO!, page 33

Go on a Polar Expedition, page 54

The red line shows their journey to eat.

The blue line shows their journey back home.

Rainforest Round-Up, page 47

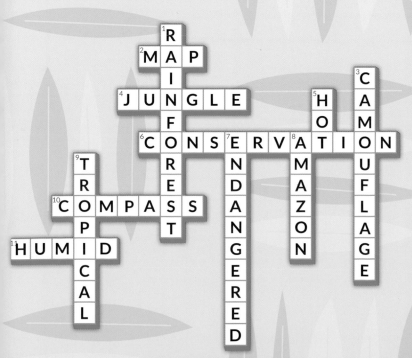

Look for your Lunch, page 66–67

C	U	R	R	Y	L	Z	K	L	Q	U	I	P	Z	A
R	E	D	D	A	H	O	I	Z	A	E	K	O	H	I
E	L	D	T	A	C	M	M	W	M	U	W	U	W	L
P	C	U	M	H	B	H	S	D	G	M	I	T	I	X
E	Q	E	A	A	W	O	H	S	U	S	H	I	B	M
T	Z	U	B	W	S	P	I	A	S	N	O	N	E	A
J	U	E	R	O	N	S	P	A	A	R	K	E	S	B
T	K	Q	C	D	U	M	P	L	I	N	G	A	A	R
F	O	A	D	T	Z	O	F	A	A	B	W	I	W	O
M	T	K	R	A	M	E	N	E	A	T	Q	N	E	R
L	A	Z	Z	C	F	T	T	S	E	U	D	N	O	F
Q	C	A	P	B	F	K	A	P	W	U	A	S	N	P
N	W	A	O	R	E	W	C	F	K	J	J	S	U	Z
T	O	R	O	N	T	P	I	Z	Z	A	P	I	A	S
F	A	J	I	T	A	C	S	X	A	B	T	A	C	W

PYRAMID SCHEME

STONEHENGE REVENGE

Start

M	J	S	D	B	L	Z	M	L	Q	U	F	G	I	G
U	E	T	O	U	H	A	I	Z	E	E	D	A	R	A	P
S	L	E	U	M	F	P	N	S	E	M	W	R	O	H
I	C	K	G	P	R	I	Z	E	S	M	R	P	I	W
E	A	C	H	E	P	O	P	C	O	Y	C	B	A	N
N	N	I	N	R	I	S	W	H	S	O	O	T	H	N
N	D	T	U	C	N	S	P	S	R	R	E	I	O	B
U	T	Q	T	A	B	T	O	N	I	R	N	C	T	R
S	O	X	S	R	Z	L	L	A	R	H	I	I	D	O
T	U	S	E	C	F	N	N	I	D	S	G	N	O	R
E	G	L	Y	V	S	O	D	T	U	O	A	D	G	G
E	I	P	D	O	D	E	U	M	W	U	M	E	S	P
W	E	N	F	E	R	R	I	S	W	H	E	E	L	Z
S	A	N	N	E	L	C	A	R	O	U	S	E	L	N
C	A	N	D	I	B	S	K	R	O	W	E	R	I	F

Bon Voyage!, pages 86–87

H E L I C O P T E R
           1   10   7

T R A I N
11 5 4

A I R P L A N E
3 12 14   9

D O G S L E D
      6   8

B I C Y C L E
13   2

UNSCRAMBLE THE SECRET MESSAGE

P L A N   A   G R E A T   T R I P !
1 2 3 4   5   6 7 8 9 10   11 12 13 14

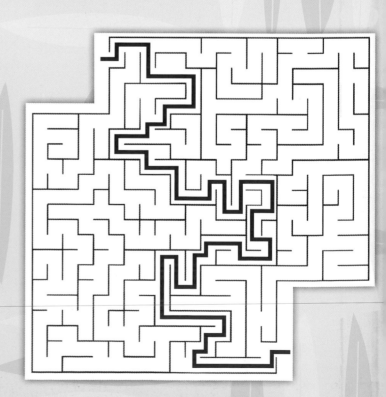

ACKNOWLEDGEMENTS

Front Cover © Maciej Czekajewski–Shutterstock.com, © Africa Studio–Shutterstock.com; **Back Cover** © Michael Kraus–Shutterstock.com, (bl) Annabella Charles Photography; **IFC** © Daniel Leppens–Shutterstock.com; **2** (t) Instagram.com/sweetiecapy, (b) © Andrey Yurlov–Shutterstock.com; **2–3** (t) © Rob Hainer–Shutterstock.com, (b) © Daniel Leppens–Shutterstock.com; **3** (t) © Jag_cz–Shutterstock.com, (b) © ilikestudio–Shutterstock.com; **4** (t) © Alex Oakenman–Shutterstock.com, (b) SunglassCat; **5** (t) ChinaFotoPress/ChinaFotoPress via Getty Images, (c) Brighton Argus/Solent News/REX Shutterstock, (b) Ian Berry. www.ian-berry.com; **6** (cl) © Samuel Borges Photography–Shutterstock.com, © Npeter–Shutterstock.com, (b) © Robyn Mackenzie–Shutterstock.com; **7** © Samuel Borges Photography–Shutterstock.com; **8–9** © Stuart Pearce / Alamy Stock Photo; **9** © M L Pearson / Alamy Stock Photo; **10–11** Boaz Rottem; **12–13** IAIN WATTS/MERCURY PRESS; **13** © photoplotnikov–Shutterstock.com; **14** © R. MACKAY PHOTOGRAPHY, LLC–Shutterstock.com, © Ugorenkov Aleksandr–Shutterstock.com, © sergign–Shutterstock.com, © Nordling–Shutterstock.com, © Yurii Vydyborets–Shutterstock.com, © Luis Carlos Torres–Shutterstock.com, © SviP–Shutterstock.com, © Richard Peterson–Shutterstock.com, © mtkang–Shutterstock.com, © Javier Brosch–Shutterstock.com, © Elnur–Shutterstock.com, © Maglara–Shutterstock.com, © Javier Brosch–Shutterstock.com; **16** © cynoclub–Masterfile.com; **16–17** © Spumador–Shutterstock.com; **17** Peter Charlesworth/LightRocket via Getty Images; **18** (t) © chrisbrignell–Shutterstock.com, (b) © Minerva Studio–Shutterstock.com; **19** (t) © Deklofenak–Masterfile.com, (c) © Javier Brosch–Shutterstock.com, (b) © Milkovasa–Shutterstock.com; **20–21** @DAXON / CATERS NEWS; **23** © MANDY GODBEHEAR–Shutterstock.com; **24–25** © Henry Westheim Photography / Alamy Stock Photo; **25** (tr, cr, br) © Daniel Leppens–Shutterstock.com; **26** (cl) © yyang–Shutterstock.com, (b) © Tribune Content Agency LLC / Alamy Stock Photo; **27** (t) The Asahi Shimbun via Getty Images, (b) © jgorzynik–Shutterstock.com; **28–29** Annabella Charles Photography; **30** © Naghiyev–Shutterstock.com; **30–31** Taxi Fabric; **32** (tr) © Africa Studio–Shutterstock.com; **33** (tr) © Naghiyev–Shutterstock.com, (bl) © smej–Shutterstock.com, (bc) © saiko3p–Shutterstock.com, (bc) © Mario Savoia–Shutterstock.com, (br) © Pikoso.kz–Shutterstock.com; **34** (cl) © Rob Cousins / Alamy Stock Photo, (br) © Michael Jenner / Alamy Stock Photo; **35** (tr) © Franck Fotos / Alamy Stock Photo, (bl) © roy henderson–Shutterstock.com; **36** Bethany Clarke/Getty Images for Canal & River Trust; **37** (l) ASSOCIATED PRESS, (r) Kyodo via AP Images; **38** (t) TOBIAS SCHWARZ/AFP/Getty Images, (b) © genlock–Shutterstock.com; **38–39** (dps) © Stephanie Zieber–Shutterstock.com; **39** (t) © Bornfree–Shutterstock.com, (b) © s_bukley–Shutterstock.com; **40–41** (t, b) Photos courtesy Sheyna E. Gifford, livefrommars.life; **41** (tr) Photo courtesy of Carmel Johnston; **42** Courtesy of James Holmdahl; **42–43** (sp) © kevron2001–Masterfile.com; **43** U-PET by L&T International Group Inc.; **44** (bl) © Jurgen Freund/naturepl.com; **44–45** (dps) © Ammit Jack–Shutterstock.com; **45** (c) © Jeff Grabert–Shutterstock.com; **46** (sp) © Angel DiBilio–Shutterstock.com; **47** (tl) © Tarbell Studio Photo–Shutterstock.com, (bl, br) © Laboko–Shutterstock.com; **48–49** Images courtesy of Ocean Sole, http://www.ocean-sole.com; **50** (b) Kakslauttanen Arctic Resort. www.kakslauttanen.fi. Photographer Valtteri Hirvonen; **50–51** © Atiketta Sangasaeng–Shutterstock.com; **51** (b) Kakslauttanen Arctic Resort. www.kakslauttanen.fi; **52–53** © Volt Collection–Shutterstock.com; **53** (tl) © Mega Pixel–Shutterstock.com, (tr) © Zoltan Major–Shutterstock.com, (b) © Mega Pixel–Shutterstock.com; **54** © Kotomiti Okuma–Shutterstock.com; **55** © Shchipkova Elena–Shutterstock.com; **56–57** Instagram.com/sweetiecapy; **58** (b) © murphy81–Shutterstock.com; **58–59** © allx–Masterfile.com; **59** (tr) © pirke–Shutterstock.com, (bl) © Ignatius Sariputra–Shutterstock.com; **60** Photo Credits: Dianne de Las Casas; **61** (tr) © Valentyn Volkov–Shutterstock.com, (bl) © Subbotina Anna–Shutterstock.com; **62** Photo Credits: Dianne de Las Casas; **62–63** © Jag_cz–Shutterstock.com; **64** © Susan Schmitz–Shutterstock.com; **64–65** © andrey_kuzmin–Masterfile.com; **65** © rprongjai–Shutterstock.com; **66** (b) © strfox–Masterfile.com; **66–67** (c) © Jose Ignacio Soto–Shutterstock.com, (b) © jamdesign–Masterfile.com; **67** (tr) © Andrey Yurlov–Shutterstock.com, (br) © UbjsP–Shutterstock.com; **69** (t) © robertosch–Masterfile.com, (b) © magann–Masterfile.com; **70** (t) Fairfax Media via Getty Images, (b) Max Mumby/Indigo/Getty Images; **71** kohlermedia.ch; **72** (b) © ilikestudio–Shutterstock.com; **72–73** SkyHighStudios/Getty Images; **73** (b) © Abel Tumik–Shutterstock.com, (b) © somyot pattana–Shutterstock.com; **74** © Alena Ozerova–Shutterstock.com; **75** © pbombaert–Shutterstock.com; **76** (l) Henryk T. Kaiser/REX/Shutterstock; **76–77** Henryk T. Kaiser/REX/Shutterstock; **78** (cr) © Rob Hainer–Shutterstock.com, (br) © isselee–Masterfile.com; **78–79** (t) © FiledIMAGE–Shutterstock.com; **79** (tr) © isselee–Masterfile.com; **80** (b) Cem Oksuz/Anadolu Agency/Getty Images; **80–81** (dps) © michelangeloop–Shutterstock.com; **81** (t) © GTS Productions–Shutterstock.com; **82** (b) © Michael Kraus–Shutterstock.com; **82–83** (dps) Roland Seitre/Minden Pictures; **83** (b) LYNN CAMPBELL / CATERS NEWS; **85** (tl) © Jagodka–Shutterstock.com, (br) © norikko–Shutterstock.com; **93** © Maciej Czekajewski–Shutterstock.com; © Africa Studio–Shutterstock.com; **MASTER GRAPHICS** © Maciej Czekajewski–Shutterstock.com

Key: t = top, b = bottom, c = center, l = left, r = right, sp = single page, bkg = background

All other photos are from Ripley Entertainment Inc.

Every attempt has been made to acknowledge correctly and contact copyright holders, and we apologise in advance for any unintentional errors or omissions, which will be corrected in future editions.